VOL. 17

CONTENTS

Ukulele performed by Chris Kringel

ISBN 978-1-4584-1877-7

7777 W. BLUEMOUND RD. P.O. BOX 13819 MILWAUKEE, WI 53213

Visit Hal Leonard Online at
www.halleonard.com

Every Breath You Take

Music and Lyrics by Sting

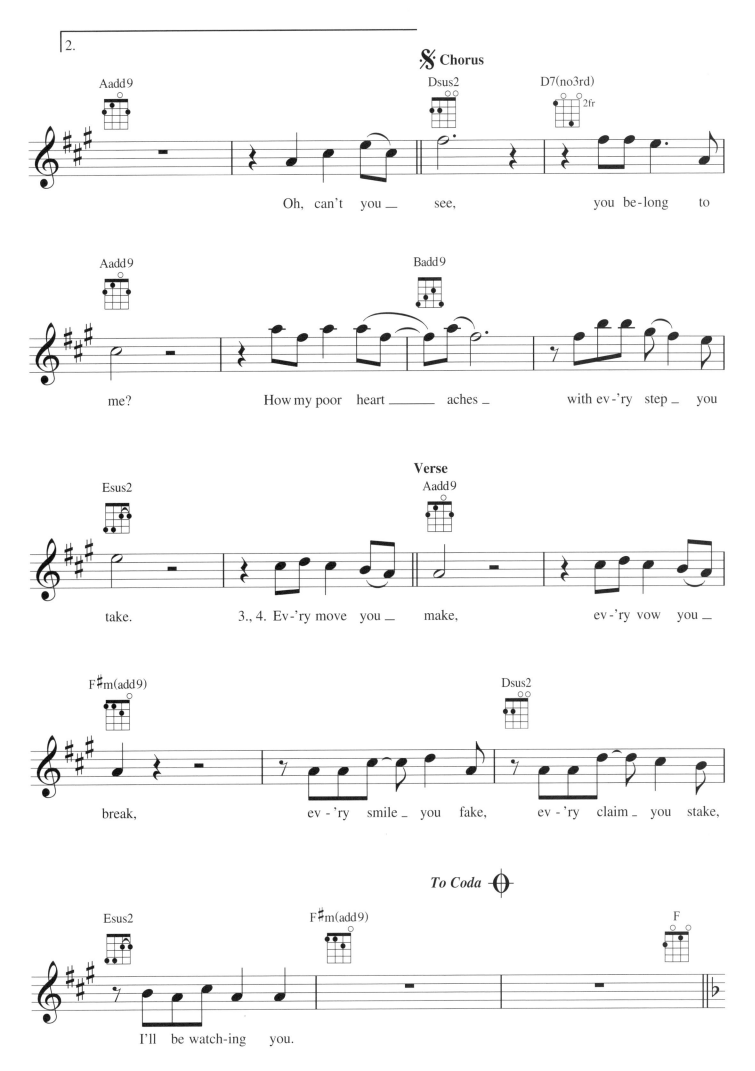

Bridge

Since you've gone, __ I've been lost _____ with - out _____ a trace.

I dream at night I can on - ly see _____ your face.

I look a - round, but it's you I can't __ re - place. I feel so cold and I

long for your __ em - brace. I keep cry - ing, ba - by, ba - by, please. __

Interlude

Aadd9   F#m(add9)   Dsus2   Esus2

F#m(add9)   Aadd9   F#m(add9)

Ooh. __   Ooh. __   Ooh. __

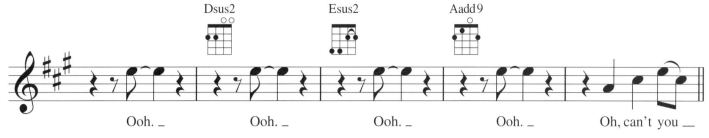

Ooh. _   Ooh. _   Ooh. _   Ooh. _   Oh, can't you _

Coda

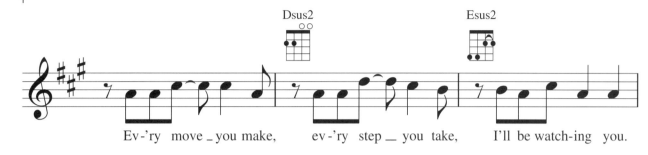

Ev-'ry move _ you make,   ev-'ry step _ you take,   I'll be watch-ing you.

I'll be watch - ing

Outro

you.
1., 5. (Ev - 'ry breath _ you take,   ev - 'ry move _ you make,
2., 4., 6., 8. (Ev - 'ry sin - gle day,   ev - 'ry word _ you say,
3., 7. (Ev - 'ry move _ you make,   ev - 'ry vow _ you break,

Repeat and fade

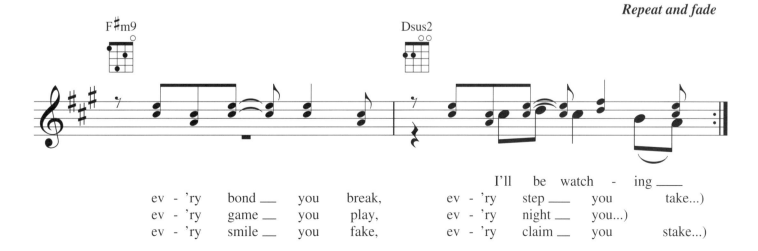

I'll be watch - ing _

ev - 'ry bond _ you break,   ev - 'ry step _ you take...)
ev - 'ry game _ you play,   ev - 'ry night _ you...)
ev - 'ry smile _ you fake,   ev - 'ry claim _ you stake...)

Fields of Gold

Music and Lyrics by Sting

TRACK 3

First note

First note

1., 2., 3. | **4.**

Intro
Moderately ♩ = 105

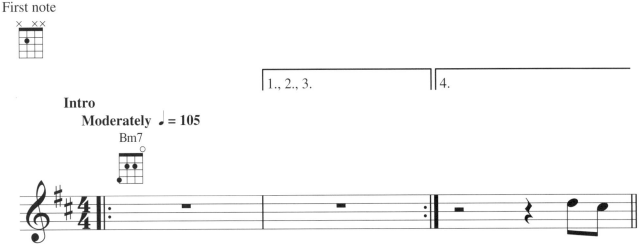

1. You'll re -

Verse

mem-ber me,   when the   west wind   moves __   up - on the fields __   of bar-
stay with me,   will you   be my   love __   a - mong the fields __   of bar-

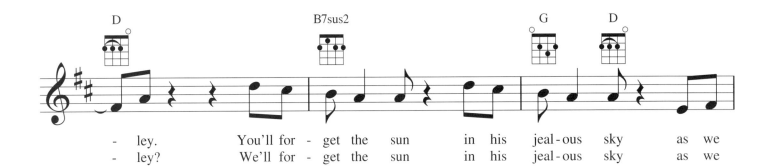

- ley.   You'll for - get the sun   in his jeal-ous sky   as we
- ley?   We'll for - get the sun   in his jeal-ous sky   as we

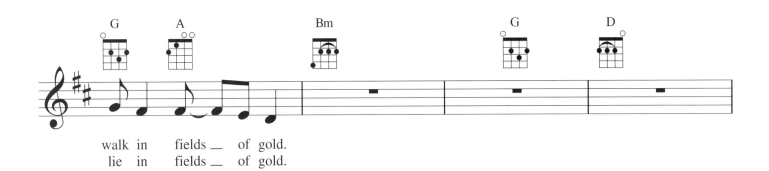

walk in   fields __ of gold.
lie in   fields __ of gold.

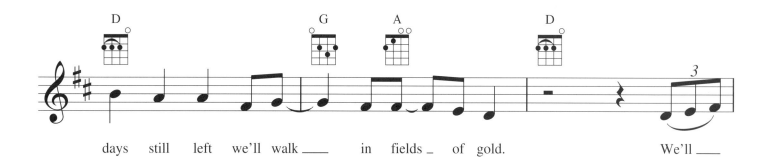

days still left we'll walk ___ in fields _ of gold. We'll ___

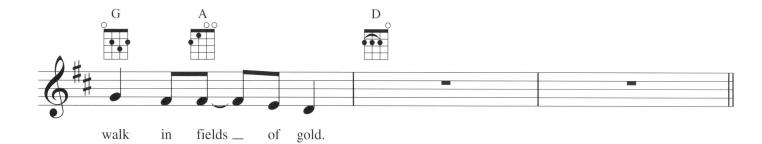

walk in fields _ of gold.

Interlude

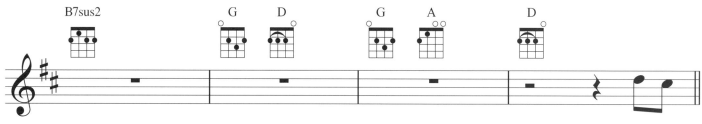

5. Man - y

Verse

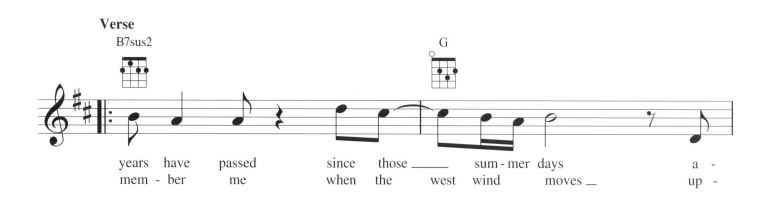

years have passed since those _____ sum - mer days a -
mem - ber me when the west wind moves ___ up -

I Just Called to Say I Love You

Words and Music by Stevie Wonder

Additional Lyrics

4. No Libra sun; no Halloween;
   No giving thanks to all the Christmas joy you bring.
   But what it is, though old so new
   To fill your heart like no three words could ever do.

Kansas City

Words and Music by Jerry Leiber and Mike Stoller

Killing Me Softly with His Song

Words by Norman Gimbel
Music by Charles Fox

TRACK 9

Intro-Chorus
Slowly, in 2 ♩ = 60

Strum-min' my pain ___ with his fin - gers, ___

sing-in' my life ___ with his words. ___ Kill-ing me soft - ly with his ___

___ song, kill-ing me soft - ly with his ___ song, tell-in' my whole ___

___ life with his ___ words, kill-ing me soft - ly ___

with his song. _____

Interlude

| C | D7 | C | D7 |

Verse

Am   D7   G

1. I heard he sang _____ a good _ song, _____   I _____ heard he
2. I felt all flushed _ with fe - ver, _____   em - bar - rassed _
3. He sang as if _____ he knew _ me _____   in _____ all _ my _____

Cmaj7   Am   D7

had a style, _____   and so I came _____ to see _ him to
_____ by the _ crowd. _   I felt he found _____ my let - ters and
_____ dark de - spair, _____   and then he looked _____ right through me as

Em   Am

lis - ten _____ for a while. _   And there _____ he was, _
read each _ one out _____ loud. _   I prayed _ that he _____
if I _____ was - n't there. _____   And he _____ just kept _

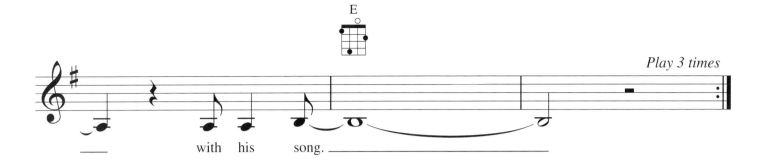

Play 3 times

with his song.

Bridge

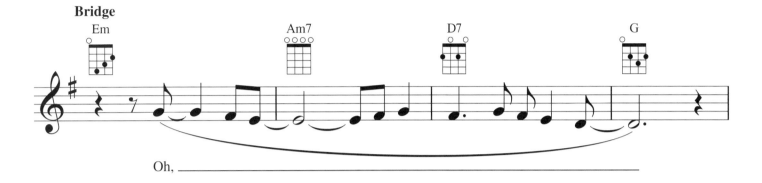

Oh,

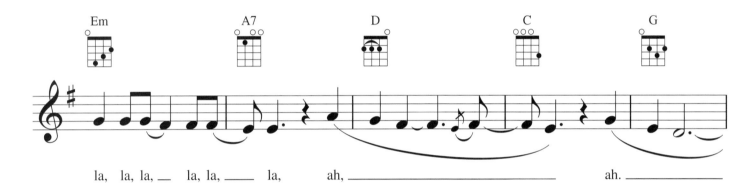

la, la, la, la, la, la, ah, ah.

D.S. al Coda

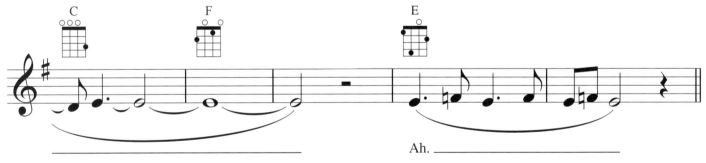

Ah.

Coda

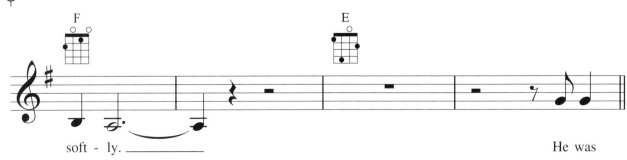

soft - ly. He was

Outro-Chorus

TRACK 11

Sunny

Words and Music by Bobby Hebb

First note

Verse
Moderately ♩ = 124

Em   G7

1. Sun - ny,   yes - ter - day my
2. Sun - ny,   thank you for the

C   F#m   B7   Em

life   was   filled   with   rain. _____   Sun - ny,
sun - shine   bou - quet. _____   Sun - ny,

G7   C   F#m   B7

you smiled   at me ____ and real - ly eased   the   pain. ___   Now the
thank you for the   love   you brought my   way. ___   You

Em   G7

dark days   are   done ____ and   the   bright days   are   here. ___
gave   to   me ____   your   all   and   all ____   and

My sun-ny one ___ shines so sin-cere.
now I feel ___ ten feet tall. ___ Sun-ny one so

Sun-ny one so

1.

true, I love you. _____

2.

true, I love you. _____

Verse

3. Sun-ny, thank you for the truth you've let me see. ___

_____ Sun-ny, thank you for the

facts from __ A to Z. ___ My life was torn __ like

wind-blown sand, _ then a rock was formed when we held hands. _

Sun-ny one so true, I love ___ you. ___

Verse

4. Sun - ny, thank you for that smile _ up - on your _ face, _

___ mm. ___ Sun - ny, thank you, thank you for

that gleam   that flows   with   grace. ___   You're   my   spark   of

na - ture's _   fire; __   you're   my   sweet   com   -   plete   de   -   sire. __

Sun - ny   one __   so   true, _____   yes,   I   love _   you. _____

Verse

5. Sun - ny, _____   yes - ter - day   all   my

Tears in Heaven

Words and Music by Eric Clapton and Will Jennings

1., 4. Would you know my name
2. Would you hold my hand

if I saw you in heav - en?
if I saw you in heav - en?

Would { it / you } be the same
Would ya help me stand

if I saw you in heav - en?
if I saw you in heav - en?

have ya beg - gin', please, ___ beg - gin' please. _____

Guitar Solo

D.S. al Coda
(take 1st ending)

Coda

Outro

en. ___ 'Cause I know I don't be - long ___

rit.

___ here in heav - en.

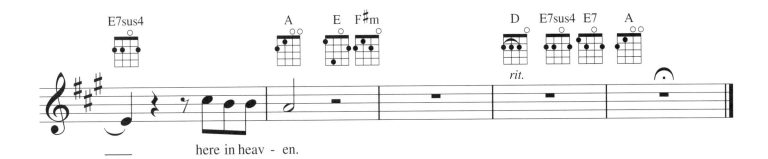

What a Wonderful World

Words and Music by George David Weiss and Bob Thiele

TRACK 15

HAL·LEONARD UKULELE PLAY-ALONG

Now you can play your favorite songs on your uke with great-sounding backing tracks to help you sound like a bona fide pro!

1. POP HITS
American Pie • Copacabana (At the Copa) • Crocodile Rock • Kokomo • Lean on Me • Stand by Me • Twist and Shout • What the World Needs Now Is Love.
00701451 Book/CD Pack.........................$14.99

2. UKE CLASSICS
Ain't She Sweet • Five Foot Two, Eyes of Blue (Has Anybody Seen My Girl?) • It's Only a Paper Moon • Living in the Sunlight, Loving in the Moonlight • Pennies from Heaven • Tonight You Belong to Me • Ukulele Lady • When I'm Cleaning Windows.
00701452 Book/CD Pack.........................$12.99

3. HAWAIIAN FAVORITES
Aloha Oe • Blue Hawaii • HarborLights • The Hawaiian Wedding Song (Ke Kali Nei Au) • Mele Kalikimaka • Sleepy Lagoon • Sweet Someone • Tiny Bubbles.
00701453 Book/CD Pack.........................$12.99

4. CHILDREN'S SONGS
Do-Re-Mi • The Hokey Pokey • It's a Small World • My Favorite Things • Puff the Magic Dragon • Sesame Street Theme • Splish Splash • This Land Is Your Land.
00701454 Book/CD Pack.........................$12.99

5. CHRISTMAS SONGS
Do You Hear What I Hear • Feliz Navidad • Frosty the Snow Man • Here Comes Santa Claus (Right down Santa Claus Lane) • Jingle-Bell Rock • Nuttin' for Christmas • Rudolph the Red-Nosed Reindeer • Santa Claus Is Comin' to Town.
00701696 Book/CD Pack.........................$12.99

6. LENNON & McCARTNEY
And I Love Her • Day Tripper • Here, There and Everywhere • Hey Jude • Let It Be • Norwegian Wood (This Bird Has Flown) • Nowhere Man • Yesterday.
00701723 Book/CD Pack.........................$12.99

7. DISNEY FAVORITES
Alice in Wonderland • The Bare Necessities • Candle on the Water • Chim Chim Cher-ee • A Dream Is a Wish Your Heart Makes • Mickey Mouse March • Supercalifragilisticexpialidocious • Under the Sea.
00701724 Book/CD Pack.........................$12.99

8. CHART HITS
All the Right Moves • Bubbly • Hey, Soul Sister • I'm Yours • Toes • Use Somebody • Viva la Vida • You're Beautiful.
00701745 Book/CD Pack.........................$14.99

9. THE SOUND OF MUSIC
Climb Ev'ry Mountain • Do-Re-Mi • Edelweiss • Maria • My Favorite Things • Sixteen Going on Seventeen • Something Good • The Sound of Music.
00701784 Book/CD Pack.........................$12.99

11. CHRISTMAS STRUMMING
Away in a Manger • Deck the Hall • The First Noel • Hark! the Herald Angels Sing • Jingle Bells • Joy to the World • O Come, All Ye Faithful (Adeste Fideles) • We Three Kings of Orient Are.
00702458 Book/CD Pack.........................$12.99

13. UKULELE SONGS
Daughter • Dream a Little Dream of Me • Elderly Woman Behind the Counter in a Small Town • Last Kiss • More ThanYou Know • Sleepless Nights • Tonight You Belong to Me • Yellow Ledbetter.
00702599 Book/CD Pack.........................$12.99

14. JOHNNY CASH
Cry, Cry, Cry • Daddy Sang Bass • Folsom Prison Blues • Hey, Porter • I Walk the Line • Jackson • (Ghost) Riders in the Sky (A Cowboy Legend) • Ring of Fire.
00702615 Book/CD Pack $14.99

15. COUNTRY CLASSICS
Achy Breaky Heart (Don't Tell My Heart) • Chattahoochee • Crazy • King of the Road • Rocky Top • Tennessee Waltz • You Are My Sunshine • Your Cheatin' Heart.
00702834 Book/CD Pack.........................$12.99

16. STANDARDS
Ain't Misbehavin' • All of Me • Beyond the Sea • Georgia on My Mind • Mister Sandman • Moon River • That's Amoré (That's Love) • Unchained Melody.
00702835 Book/CD Pack.........................$12.99

17. POP STANDARDS
Every Breath You Take • Fields of Gold • I Just Called to Say I Love You • Kansas City • Killing Me Softly with His Song • Sunny • Tears in Heaven • What a Wonderful World.
00702836 Book/CD Pack.........................$12.99

23. TAYLOR SWIFT
Crazier • Fearless • Love Story • Mean • Our Song • Teardrops on My Guitar • White Horse • You Belong with Me.
00704106 Book/CD Pack.........................$14.99

HAL·LEONARD® CORPORATION
7777 W. BLUEMOUND RD. P.O. BOX 13819 MILWAUKEE, WI 53213

www.halleonard.com
Prices, contents, and availability subject to change without notice.
Disney characters and artwork © Disney Enterprises, Inc.